On the Loose

CULTURAL
CENTER
OF CAPE COD

All the Arts for All of Us

On the Loose

POEMS BY

Judith Askew

Bass River Press
South Yarmouth, Massachusetts

Copyright © 2016 by Judith Askew
All rights reserved

No part of this book may be reproduced, stored in a database or other retrieval system, or transmitted in any form, by any means, including mechanical, electronic, photocopy, recording or otherwise, without the prior written permission of the publisher.

Printed by IngramSpark (Lightning Source, Inc.)
Edited by Angela Howes
Interior Design and Composition by Angela Howes
Cover art by Rebecca Strohm

Published by Bass River Press
307 Old Main St.
South Yarmouth, MA 02664
www.cultural-center.org

An imprint of the Cultural Center of Cape Cod, Bass River Press was created to support literary artists from the Cape & Islands. Award-winning poet Tony Hoagland judged the press's first poetry competition and selected Judith Askew's collection from a very impressive field of submissions.

Library of Congress Control Number: 2015958567

This publication was made possible by the Friends of South Yarmouth Library Association and a grant from the Mid-Cape Cultural Council, a local agency which is supported by the Massachusetts Cultural Council, a state agency.

for Hugh

Acknowledgements

So many people have been supportive and helpful to me in the vibrant poetry community on Cape Cod. I would particularly like to thank poet and judge Tony Hoagland for selecting *On the Loose*, and Lauren Wolk for her leadership in all the arts and especially for her work in envisioning this press for the poets of Cape Cod, long a dream of ours. And a big thank you to Editor Angela Howes for her creativity, attentiveness, and good sense in the assembly of this book. A warm note of gratitude to the Steeple Street Poets for their sharp critical eyes and discerning comments. And thank you to Greg Hischak, Christine Rathbun Ernst, Alice Kociemba, Barry Hellman, John Bonanni, and Gemma Leghorn for providing venues where poetry can be heard, read, or discussed here on the Cape.

CONTENTS

Living without a To-Do List	11
Adages	12
The young girls' latest fad	13
Hair	14
Coming of Age	15
Secrets	16
Happy birthday	17
Sex	18
Homage to the Pill	19
Shadows on the Screen	20
If only	21
Caesar Musing after Meeting Cleopatra	22
Warrior	23
Flying Blind	24
Unusual Meeting	25
You're too much work	26
The Greening of America	29
Carnival on Wall Street	30
Bakery of Lies	31
Buried Treasure	32
Catastrophic Expectations	34
An English Teacher's Lament	35
Expression on Time's Face	36
Moments	37
Memory, Fact, Story, Loss	39
The Unhistorical Clothes Pin	40
A Protestant Mourns Sensations Lost	45
Homage: Rock, the Park	47
Come, See	48
Windy Day, Tennessee Valley Trail	49
Aromatherapy	50
Pink and Blue Dawn	52
"Finish Your Milk"	53
Baby Talk	54
The Future	55
On the Loose	56
Mowing the Lawn	57
Orleans Parade, July 4	59
A Swan Song for Shoestring Bay	61
Voice from the Grave	62

I

Living without a To-Do List

I've always had difficulty staying on Earth
tethered to the here and now.
I go romping off into sky,
a frequent flyer into spacey thoughts.

Be happy, I write in my journal. *Stay engaged. Exercise.*
Everyone recommends exercise for everything—
brain function, figure, balancing moods.

Sometimes I go for walks into the sunset.
I had a favorite walk in San Francisco.

I didn't need to write it on my to-do list:
walk to the Marina, face
the Golden Gate Bridge, walk into the sky
of spilled cranberry orange juice.

A life without lists—say one with flow—
might lead to a break-out,
to looking into the eyes of a stranger
to connect.

Hugh said, *Do what you want.* He was Jewish
and I was Methodist. And we both made lists.

In the morning he made a list that filled
a whole page in a notebook.

I knew he was doing what he wanted,
while Mother's voice echoed inside:
Tidy the porch where you left a mess.

Tidy... has gone on 10,017 lists.

At the end of the month, Hugh skimmed
his lists to be sure nothing was missed.
Then he started a new notebook.

That's even more methodical than the Methodist.
I'll let my body remember what's important.

Adages

Surprisingly, I don't fall into complete
   torpor and sloth
when I begin to remove the staples

of adages my parents impressed
   into me, stitches they hoped
would dress me in responsibility

and a white bridal gown. It took
   years of picking away at them
like removing ticks from a dog.

By the time I understood a stitch
   in time saves nine, my mother
sat entranced by TV, her mending

egg and sock held motionless,
   upright in her hand like Liberty's
torch. As for a place for everything,

my mind, not to mention my home,
   was cluttered with satisfying
jumbles piled here and there,

which gives the lie to less is more,
   and I must say the grass is always
greener in a city where nonstop

intoxication lures. "Happiness lies
   in fewness of wants," Grandad instructed,
turning me into a poet, skimpy

in conventional desire and rich
   in a search for Truth.
I do save pennies, for rainy days come

often, but sometimes putting off
   until tomorrow the ordinary things
of today—yields sumptuous diversions.

The young girls' latest fad

appears, a thing of beauty: turquoise and blues, aqua
and sequins and sparkles, something
she pulls on over a swimsuit
then slips smoothly into a pool.

In her mermaid tail, a birthday gift—
the only one she wanted—
she surprises even her reluctant parents
with her grace and loveliness.
They show off pictures of her
as though they can't quite believe
what they've created.

The young mermaid posts the images
and soon collects a school of mermaid friends
who revel in this new twist on an old tale
of sylphs who sit on sea rocks in the distance
where they comb their golden hair or flash
attached to the backs of dolphins.

Her imagination is stimulated by a local artist
who painted only naiads bare-breasted at the stove
or on the beach frolicking with sailors
or wearing pearls and hats to church.
On school visits, he explains his fetish ladies
as mermaidens growing up, innocent beauties
who glide and slide without feet to stand on,
creatures in the dreams of young men.

Why, she asked her mother, *do we love
our mermaid tails?* Her mother grimaced.
It's a phase, she said. *Remember when
you were four, you would only wear pink
and insisted we call you Princess?*

Hair

A friend said: You should grow your hair long.
Oh, I thought.

It's stick straight, thick with skinny strands.
It's difficult.

It ruined my wedding. It ruined my junior prom.
If I had an excuse for my life, it ruined it.

Mother has curly hair.
It's another of my complaints against her.
She should have given me curly hair instead of pretty feet.

My plan was to coax curl into my hair.
It grew and grew, and I began to see little waves
like crimped French fries or wind-laden flags or rippling grasses.

Such long hair flows so naturally, not clipped
to precision, the vision
of the salon fascist.

It blows in the wind, shows a woman
with romantic tresses to toss this way and that,
a woman of the come-hither hair.

A woman of a certain age with short, close-cropped hair
lies like a fallow field out of season,

unlike the wanton young girls flipping their wild manes,
fillies of the field about to lie down in darkness

hair or no hair.

Coming of Age

i. Seeker

Her therapist called her
the faceless lady. She went home,
read Tolstoy. She asked her friend
the secret, but her friend was reading
Kill the Buddha and said there were no
secrets. She called her father.
He told her not to sell her stocks
at this time. Her acupuncturist
said it was all a matter of energy,
punctured her belly. At night
she dreamed a man came to take
her away in a limousine,
but she told him a story
instead.

ii. Wanderer

She took up space filling
all the rooms. Even at night she stole
dreams, pulling them through walls
to wind through the passages of her mind
where they drifted like smoke.
She kindled blazes, watched the fires
flare, sputter, then die out.
She wandered through rooms,
a lone tree blackened on the horizon.

iii. Dancer

She wore her boots for seven years,
rolled her cuffs, but not her joints
and her dark hair flew around the edges
where the air stood on end.

A Spanish dancer slept in her feet
and coiled in her brain a dark saloon
where her feet would know no rhythm
and her hair would know a rose.

Secrets

Twelve is the year the air fills with secrets
floating like pollen on the sunlit path
from Mother to friends. Center stage
shifts to a two-story brick school—
echoing stairwells; long corridors;
and musty corners. A gymnasium
and a locker room. Here a telltale
sign waggles tongues: no light
glints from soft hair on a shaved leg.
Before a long mirror, a borrowed lipstick
passes from trembling hand to trembling hand,
pressing brilliant color to tender lips.
Such a color would surely attract!
Repel? Who is sitting out the period?
Who undresses in a dark corner
to hide a budding breast? By spring,
each has handstitched her name
across a blue gym suit shirt pocket.

Happy birthday,

birth control pill! Thanks to you,
we had no more need to keep pants zipped,
no need to keep our panties on, our knees together.

Car bedrooms popped up behind
schools, dark golf courses, beside the lake
where the moon on water beckoned
a quiet come-to-me
soon crescendoing in full moon tumult.

I don't know why I used to cry.
Was that because it was over?
Because there were still so many *sotto voce* messages
that fluttered like butterflies
yet left the body driven to explore more virgin roads?

But the body knew:
in the hands of a prince
a slumbering beauty had been awakened;
a hundred muttering voices had been driven off,
the voices of disgrace had slinked away.

It was the end of the nuns' wicked care of teen mothers,
the end of fathers waving shotguns.
It was the beginning of mothers' deepening envy.

New concepts sprang up like fertile weeds:
Planned Parenthood, sex education,
coed dorms, and oral contraceptives.

We knew we were trial balloons sent up
in a freakish wind storm.
We entered a new geography, endured
a prescribing doctor's disdain,
and rigorously counted days

hoping our regulated uteri would start up on another day,
when the time was right
like a winterized car in a 20-degree snowstorm.

Sex,

making love, so shrouded in delicacy
and bombast, your hands, just your touch,
your arms surrounding me, enliven me.
I want to crawl all over you
begin to wrap my legs around you

energized by whatever it is—the strength,
the power, the sheer difference
of your muscles, your skin and that thing
that rises.

I suppose it is an experience
that differs so much—man to woman
woman to man—that it defies description,
an act so wonderful when it is

even poets usually refuse to detail
the nuts and bolts of it, if you'll excuse
such a general mechanical term.

But there is that feminine response,
which comes from arousal,

an interior brooklet that begins to flow.

There is no name for it—secretion, lubrication—
that *hello everything goes well here*
he sings to himself when he touches
the wetness he arouses.

So I give you a name for it:
shemanna. It's a lovely word isn't it,

companion to semen.

What is it the first time a young man
realizes he has touched honeypot, honey gold:
he is a man and this is one thing she does for him.

Homage to The Pill

If I were a sculptor
I would sculpt a circular white thing
something oversized like Oldenburg's "Clothespin"

(what human impact did the clothespin have
compared to the birth control pill?).

In most cases, a man leaves the deepest,
most frequent footprints on Earth;

he sculpts the perfect human body
and various large metal objects,

but he has not anointed The Pill
with his signature;

it's a woman thing, after all.

Or put another way for her,
it offered choice, control, consciousness.

His drive to people the Earth with his seed—
remember all those 'begats'—

was a successful project.

Now something new,
something womanly.

Shadows on the Screen

Reading a poem set in Vietnam,
my fingers begin to tingle: *I want
a cigarette?* One piece of an era
returns tightly wrapped like a pack
of smokes, those tiny requirements

for sophistication, arbiters of gender
distance, if we cared to notice then:
for her, years of posing as a screen reflection,
her cigarette balanced between two extended fingers,
nails brilliant red, while he cupped his white

cylinder between thumb and finger.
The lighting—his ever-ready Zippo—
a quick click fire. Did she gaze
mischievously into his eyes
as she inhaled smoke deep inside?

She stood, her décolleté to be admired,
smiling at his jokes, objectified and wrapped
in clear cellophane. Unknown to her
he vied with other guys to win
the prettiest girl in the room.

And so the party evening passed,
the mating hunt a diorama of approach, retreat.
The tension broken at last, we flowed into a merger,
then moved apart in the first cigarette afterwards,
passed it back and forth between the two of us.

If only,

I could eat air, make a feast of it,
flavor it with cinnamon and sugar,
grill it and listen to it hiss on the coals,
feel myself salivate, anticipate
a mouth-watering, energy-sustaining, finger-lickin' good
Thanksgiving dinner of turkey and squash.

Instead I'm eating my air full of
pockets of affirmations and low calorie bread crumbs.

When I was a teenager, pleasure was an adult concept,
a many-layered cake yet to be enjoyed,
so I sniffed the air for other possibilities and forgot to eat,
thought meals should be as simple as a hand full of grass.

Now I eat air, the hot air of gossip on the edges
of a pot luck lunch enticing with carrot sticks and hummus.

At least we don't strap ourselves into death-
defying corsets and girdles and hosiery plugged into garter belts.
Have we come a long way baby, I ask the woman selling Spanx?

Look at the Columbia Pictures lady-logo, no longer
as chubby as Marilyn Monroe. Today her arms protrude
from flapper-doo sleeves, skinny bicep bumps nearly invisible.
She couldn't grasp air, let alone survive a sneeze.

Caesar Musing after Meeting Cleopatra

That dish in Egypt, indeed!
My men call her that.
She is worthy of me, not old Antony.
Now she is a leaf in the laurel crown of Rome.

But she is too wily, too full of the joy—
is it of ruling? Does a miasma lifting
from the mysterious Nile surround her?
Perhaps she has that feeling a woman

sometimes has—not kinship affection or love
for one's people or love of spectacle, but
that devotion a woman such as Penelope
had for her wandering Odysseus.

Could she have brought such a feeling to Antony?
Well, I shall find out.
I shall take the wench to Rome,
display her like the lioness she is.

Proud woman, queen, she shall be mine.
Imagine Antony leaving the battle for her,
turning his ship around to follow. A dish, indeed.
All Rome shall feast on the sight of her.

Warrior

Hector, you in your Bronze Age finery
make quite a spectacle of yourself:
chest-covering shield and that bristling
horsehair helmet, some 70 pounds

of fiery splendor, enough to make any woman
turn her head to watch you move
through the Scaean Gates
and out to battle for the love of it,

not just for wife and child and Troy,
but for the sheer excitement, blood
lust that answers a deep move-
ment to honor, to elevate, to purchase

immortality, which it did, Hector, as I write
of you almost three millennia later,
astonished at your brawn and magnificence
outside Troy's walls year after year.

But it is your meeting with Andromache
and your startled crying son that moves
me as you remove your helmet
to stop his tears, toss him in the air,

kiss him like any modern dad,
pray he will be first in glory,
strong and brave like his father,
a joy to his mother, who begs you

not to widow her, not to leave her
alone—her mother, father, brothers
butchered—her husband so "young and warm
and strong." Ah, Hector, you of the flesh

can imagine your wife, though enslaved,
buoyed by your courage and honor
as she draws water at a well far from Troy—
believing yourselves puppets in the gods' drama

somewhere between superstition and reason,
humanity and gore.

Flying Blind

I'd love to meander your mind,
ride the roller coaster of your wit.

How I would soar. I'd barely hold
the safety bar, feet flying behind.

I'd explore the ins and outs
of your intrigues, of your self-satisfying
rendezvous hillocks, your secret bistros,

rooms where noon
slips so easily into evening
like a strap off a shoulder.

Oh the circular sweet lip of the wine glass
turns of phrases round and round.

I'd ride the air compressor bellow
to blow new meaning onto an old idea,
and spray philosophy with a patina of dust.

I'd follow your winding roads
deeper and deeper
into a sunlit forest
to end in a surprised glen;

I'd pass between the in door and the out door
of your whirlwind mind, so brilliantly limned
into new combinations, setting off bells

sounding, I swear, like the end of a war;

bells everywhere lighting up
so spontaneously, so simultaneously
ever so sweetly

to be lost in your singing mind.

Unusual Meeting

If this is to be my last day on Earth, so be it:
billowing clouds float high, the sun dazzles,
and I'm about to fly over the Rocky Mountains

to Crested Butte, a town with an unpaved
main street, ski trails, and a summer balloon festival,
a town that knows how to keep its secrets to itself.

I'm waiting at the counter for the six-seater's
ticket-taker-pilot-baggage-handler to check me in.
As instructed I ask to ride shotgun co-pilot.

The man standing next to me says,
"I was just going to ask the same question.
Look, *I* have a pilot's license."

"Go for it," I say, giving way to safety over scenery.
My quick acquiescence tweaks my fellow traveler
who follows me, protests guiltily, then flips

a coin that rolls across the vinyl floor.
Undignified in his city suit, he chases it.
"I'll take the seat on the way out," I say,

not the least bit bothered by his lack of gallantry,
for I am a modern woman—self-sufficient,
easy-going, and happy, besides.

You're too much work,

I'm sorry to say. The fact that you wear
sweat pants that flap above your ankles

with black trouser socks and business shoes—
well, you *have* learned that colorful wool sweaters

have their place anywhere. And when
I protest you say, "You deserve better"

and change—so you were not being casual, rather
lazy and insulting. I never suspect someone

will knowingly insult me by not helping
around the house or be so insecure that placing

a few dishes in the dishwasher would mean
loss of ego in your straight arm game of

one-up, one-down humor. What the hell—
why don't I give up the notion

that a relationship (watch *that* word immolate)
could be like flowers in a room,

simple existing in breeze and beauty
rather than your turn-a-chair-around,

sit backwards and spout wisdom,
which, of course, my tender hooks

of love overlook the nonsense of, smile
as though impressed, run a hand over

your slouched shoulder now ready
for a rescue of another kind, not in kind.

II

The Greening of America

Everyone needs money. Without it, you sit all day
in Union Square with a begging bowl. I used to
think the Business Roundtable—corporate Galahads
who make up rules we don't (even) know
we follow—locked us in fear and working
hard. Now I know. The economic machine has loopholes
the poor slide right through on their way to freedom.
The safety net stretches all the way from the president's
office to Congress, a kind of trampoline, where important
people jump. We don't know why. Maybe they need re-
creation. We know money can be seen in many forms:
some you wear to establish a new frontier around
yourself; some seems brought on the wind. Look
for the strings attached! No one is free from money
hunger, try as we might to bury it for some religious
treasure of humility and grace. Never mind what the mystics
say, go for it in this climate, the greening of America.
Shoeshine millionaires still shine, boat people still float
their assets across the wide ocean of despair. Try to see
America through their eyes. Watch the immigrants flow
into America like white folks who came in hope and fear
to find peaceful reds soon furious by new roadsides.
What can we do? Hispanic, Indian—you name it—
is here to stay, more greening of America.

Carnival on Wall Street
September 2008

Here we go again
riding the dream machine.

The greed game swings wildly.

We make the bell ring
at the end of the day,
at the top of the pole.

We take the Ferris ride
up, up, and around.

We put our dreams in the hands
of the carnival man
who pulls the levers, decides

when to grind the ride
to a slow, slow stop.

But the view from the top
of that dynamic machine,
that glorious lighted world of whirl,
world of wind

turns eerie:
the landscape of fall,
green dropping from trees,
red and yellow rising.

Oh, the macabre beauty of the thing.

But never mind. Come
stroll the fair ground. Come

buy some cotton candy,
the wispy, sticky, messy, melting
dream

of more, more, more
and still more.

Bakery of Lies

My favorite is the cream puff lie,
the kind inflated with hot air,
expanded to make an heroic-sized story.

Another is the cannoli, a long lie,
well-packed with nutty details,
lightly wrapped in flakey truth.

A macaroon isn't a *little* white lie,
but it's covered
with self-serving coconut.

The apple tart carries slices
of sour gossip, only
slightly sweetened with truth.

Then there's the Napoleon,
an Iago lie of pernicious intent,
layer upon layer of dark deceit.

Buried Treasure

I'm unexpectedly connected
to a familiar accent:
India. Again.

Are my outside wires wet, cross-
ed, out of sorts? I ask.

My little joke doesn't make it
over the cultural barrier.

Just a minute, she says.
It will only take a minute.

11 a.m.

Screen after screen
of dark squiggles come and go

while we search for the golden doubloon.

Just another minute, she says.
Just a minute.

She seems well informed:
click this, click that.

Now she consults a colleague.

Don't hang up, she says,
This will only take a minute.

With surprise, I realize
she's as invested as I,

who never viewed
a conversation with India
from the other side

(and I don't mean after death,
though these calls are unending).

Minutes tick away.

Now I fall on my knees,
crawl under my desk,
reboot the router:

Aaaaah! A flashing green light!

Applause breaks out in the background
and I imagine my navigator
has guided her first lost one
back to shore.

I tell her it's just in time
for my lunch.

What about you? I ask.

It's 10 p.m. in India, she says.
We go home now.

Catastrophic Expectations

When I watch the woman at the beach read on her Kindle,
a flood tide sweeps me up, rolls over a lifetime
of reading books, losing and finding them,
even turning pages, quick lick of a digit—

all lost, were I to read by Kindle.

No more forgotten loaned and borrowed books
that wash up on shore in a wave of apologies.

Kindle isn't quite the invention of electricity or the automobile,
but still to us literary types it's a surfboard of alarm.

No longer merged mind to mind on the calm Sea of Gutenberg,
I fear being locked out instead of logged on,
my desired book adrift in cyberspace.

All my cartons of books carefully packed, shipped city to city,
give way to one gilt-edged, velvet-lined box
cradling Kindle.

Would anyone want my treasures?
My menopause books, Jung, A Child's Garden of Verses?

Maybe the Italians will dismantle the mountains of discarded
		books,
build another hotel like the one they built
of 12 tons of trash picked up on European beaches.

I could go to Rome, read *Moby Dick* on my hotel wall

while here at home, walls will be walls;
bookshelves will disappear like the lost city of Atlantis,

and late afternoon bookstore meanderings
will be just a computer click away.

I'd want to move my reading chair away from the window—
too much light on the screen.

An English Teacher's Lament

I slice and dice my raspberry Jello while I watch
the latest phenom celeb, a young English chef,
convince the LA school board
to deep-six chocolate and strawberry sugar milk
that props kids up all afternoon
in recess-less classes.

We deserve better, he tells the mothers
dressed as asparagus and radishes
rallied to consult the education czars
who cancel the meeting to avoid
talking healthy food to a garden of protesting heads.

The obese schoolchildren's art and music
has already been deep-sixed out tall classroom windows
where students in other times gazed
daydreaming about their futures.

Now the LA school board thinks it could save money,
get better results by placing students in dark interiors,
have them learn science and math and engineering—
online, perhaps?—
be better trained to march
as a cohort straight into corporate cubicles.

Expression on Time's Face

Time-honored, the face of time grows wrinkles:
first, a shadow falls across grass,
then an hour glass drops minutes, grain by grain.
Somewhere a watch keeper calls out the hours.

Soon the moon's face beams around
the corners of one day, one night:
the sun's shadow counted out by twelve.
Now digital in all its blinking presence—

endless time, neither day nor night, linear—
merging night with day, confusing
our senses, waking sleep, sleeping awake.
At one time, steeple hours rang merrily,

reverberating among trees. In a distant Orient
culture, each hour a new fragrance wafted:
a scent of lily, of hyacinth, of rose,
of citrus, of lemon, of sage,

contriving a garden of hours,
a day of small gain, a day of great pleasure.

Moments

i. Edward Hopper's "Office at Night, 1940"

Each person and object in the room stands out
starkly alone. One window is closed, the other
open and filled by Hopper's inevitable

breathing shade. The light lies, an odd
intruder, another character in this scene
of barrier, inhibition, restraint—or is it

anticipation? The woman in her very tight
blue dress turns from the open file drawer
with a tiny smile as she looks toward

a paper on the floor. Or is she peeking at the man
behind the desk holding a report unnaturally upright?
Will they collide awkwardly, both springing

at once to pick up the paper, warm hands
touching, his tie so straight,
her stockings and heels shaping her legs just so?

ii. My Office, 1990

By this time offices are frenzied:
stacked papers pile on every surface, men
answer their own phones, windows clamp

tightly shut. Once, down into my 17th floor
view, a window washer silently glided,
dangling boots, then knees, then the scaffold

where he sat sweeping his arms like a snow angel,
clearing swaths of sparkling glass through his soapy
scrim. I jumped up, pretended to trace

hello on my side of the barrier, greeting him
as he slid by, his airborne seat and skyward ways
rigidly controlled by distant machinery.

He didn't even smile. He, his bucket, squeegee
and sponge disappeared as suddenly as they appeared,
like a song from a passing car window.

Memory, Fact, Story, Loss
for silversmith John Carey

Around these gifts—this shawl, these blue French plates, this
    pendant
that encloses the stars in the night—the sense
of the giver hovers like a mist still whispering over a river
at dawn. The giver remembers the thought, the shopping, the
    presentation and response.

And the one who receives the shawl, the plates, or the pendant
holds the giver in memory, where the two of them float
like swans on a river.

But the artifact is more than the gift and its lingering aura.
A story arises how the pendant was fashioned from slag pile
shards a boy and girl gathered, their father remembering
the son's excited *I found one* as later he turns the bits of color
in heat, imagines the melting swirl soon to be contained
in the pendant's silver casing.

And so the material of the world becomes entangled
with memory, with story, with art,
for the pendant came to grace the neck of a woman in a
    photograph
who embraces her first child, his chubby hand reaching for it.

In a virtual world where images flash like light reflecting
on a river's moving water, a world without memory
or substance, a world without story or art, the shawl,
the blue French plates, and the pendant are drawn up
into the eye of a cyclone, into a circle of flying debris.

The Unhistorical Clothes Pin

Claes Oldenburg sculpted one.
It stood forty-five feet tall,
resembled a man striding across a park
proclaiming ownership and exploration,
definitely not care and coziness,
as pins will do holding the wash to a line,
stitching together the family sheets and shirts,
so swiftly gathered in when raindrops sputter.

Soon we who know such things will pass
and who will care
except antique dealers and historians,
who don't much care about such women things,
things like what a family ate for dinner
or how best to teach a child to tie a shoe,
or what these small wooden pincer things held together.

Bless mothers, their knobby fingers
that smoothed the blanket
of a well-made bed, clipped
the undershirts and undershorts to the line,
proclaiming a well-made family
for all the neighbors to observe:
how the wash went out every Monday,
how many sheets and shorts,
aprons and shirts danced and flapped.

Robert Bly wrote a poem, "Clothespins"
(which started my meditation).
He spelled it (correctly) as one word
so that another word *spins*
reminds me how clothes tumble
in a line of clothes dryers
that burn shirts, pull spring out of waist bands
and rumple everything,
even snuff the deep fluff from towels.
Does he know such things?

He knows the sweet smell of wind and sunshine
in a sheet that flew all day from the clothesline.
(Or how satisfied a husband feels
to carve a clothespin for his wife.)

Some hardware stores with wooden floors
still stock clothes pins and rope
to stretch between trees or poles
or from apartment pulley to apartment pulley.
Grandmother Askew leaned out the bathroom window
to hang her wash, pulling each gleaming white item
from the high pile in the tin basin
at her feet, the line soon droopy with sheets.
Grandmother Stiles' children counted the linen napkins
the laundry man picked up each Monday morning.
And so the laundry tells a little story
of two sets of grandparents—
and some tension in a family history.

One day in San Francisco, in a neighbor's yard
from a clothesline (no longer there)
strung from a back porch to a tree
hung four sets of gloves clipped
in matched pairs: grey, white, brown, and blue,
an image of order that haunts me still.

Now our neighbor across Jones Street
washes one brassiere each Tuesday (a rebel)
and hangs it inside all day to dry
from a wire coat hanger (another disappearing artifact).
It's our private joke, our weekly calendar.
We don't know the woman, but one Tuesday
she will miss and we will wonder
how sick she is. She will pass, too,
like the clothes pins,
right out of history, silently,
from Jones Street, from her window.

III

A Protestant Mourns Sensations Lost

*The greatest poverty is not living
in a physical world.* —Wallace Stevens

Thirteen years *perfect attendance*
in Sunday School, a pall of reticence
surrounded each joy of ice cream cone;
my youthful interior streets
lost in the mystery of waiting, of love,
of service. Did such ruminations
make the cold sweeter? A philosopher
would know, stroking keys in thoughtful
pursuit of a perfect reason expressed
in perfect harmonies to a perfect
receiving mind, if only one knew enough,
read enough, thought deeply enough,
studied enough, praised God
enough.

London's new wheel, an ever-present
reminder of the underlying order of
proteins, so interlocking, so irreducible,
so dazzlingly perfect that surely a Prime
Thinker started it all rolling; no haphazard,
fly-by-night imperfect Creator
who pulled off God's socks to tweak His toes.
No, this Creator knows why 99.99% of all species
are extinct. And this brings me to the lovely world,
the flowering fruit trees, white lace lightly
stitched to limb. Surely if you listen,
petals softly chime. Or look, cherry pom-poms cluster,
a glorious overpopulated world tree, where so many
vibrating groups cling, until a breeze draws them away,
to fall like an angel's tiny crystal raindrops of raspberry tears.
Look, there the wind, there the carpet of tears.
Gone, gone for another spring.
Or the umbrella cherry, perfect strings of dangling gems,
its shape a mystery of protection, of lovers holding
hands, of a quiet, perfect Japanese courtship
here in my cousin's garden, the tree given by her friends,
a wedding gift they planted beside the front door,

the older women's wisdom marking spring, young love,
marrying the symbol to the quivering blossoms,
this plant-poem blooming faithfully,
growing like their lives held in the world glory
of each perfect spring explosion, each tree playing
its part in the annual awakening that for a week or two—
such economy—raises a crescendo so lovely
one bears its transition only by turning
to the now-fragrant, thrusting lilacs, the drooping wisteria.
One accepts the perfect great round, the maypole
dance, the orange blossom crown, the Ferris wheel
of Time.

Homage: Rock, the Park

Before *national park*
or even a city's central carpet of green grass and trees
entered anyone's imagination,

a young man dreamed
on his European tour
in the manicured, flowered, and fountained
public gardens

of something new, something sublime—
landscape parks he would design
for New World natural connection.

Genius of place,
he envisioned plots of rolling land,
of rough woods, of outcrops of rocks,
of streams and mountains—

America's wild expanses, domesticated.

Preserver of place: Central Park in midtown;
the Fenway—weeds, marsh and all;
Yosemite; and a site for Chicago's World's Fair.
Stanford, Cornell, Manhattanville.

Even in a Cape Cod village,
a home called Fernbrook
sheltered by oaks.

Frederick Law Olmsted invented *landscape design*
to protect us from our greed,
though it cost him his sanity.

Come, See

Come, see, for
  spring is near-
ly...hear the chirp
  chirrup of the
song sparrows
  in the trembling
petals on the ground
  a tightly curled

orange pop-
  py bud. Come,
watch, it will toss
  its green cap
up to heaven
  when the warm
breath of spring
  kisses it open.

Windy Day
Tennessee Valley Trail

Just before the tall grasses flare
out to meet the beach,

where the sluice pond
huddles at the head of the valley,

seagulls fly frantically,
tread exuberantly in air.

Each bird takes off,
wheels in a half circle, attempts
to fly back into the valley.

They are not speckled young gulls
strengthening their wings
or learning to fly.

In the pond below,
white flashes dip in and out,
throw sparkles to the wind.
Some birds float with ruffled feathers
on the rumpled water.

I stand transfixed.

Where is the gull's clamor,
its lusty scamper for food?

Who would think that seagulls play?

Aromatherapy
Blossom Trail, Fresno, California
April

No orange blossom world swirled;
   only ponderous fruit
clustered tree after tree,

row after row.
   Some may have rotted
on the ground, orange on brown.

To my city-starved eyes,
   they glowed, more bountiful
than grocery mounds.

Along we rolled in our air-
   conditioned car, drenching
our sight full. I cried: *Look.*

Herons. We stopped. Opened the door.
   My city-starved nostrils filled
with citrus fragrance,

palpable and warm with the gardens
   of Eden, Babylon and Rumi
singing his poetry. Was it sight, smell,

taste, or sound that whirled before me
   rising with the memory of orange
blossoms I carried the day I married,

a day stretching to an open future
   full of spring times,
expectant and enticing?

O devastating, overwhelming, intoxicating
   fragrant and everlasting
orange blossom perfume,

soaking the air, soaking my city soul.
   I blessed life. I blessed love.
I blessed the orange blossoms

no longer there, their fragrance
  a signature, an offspring,
an annual renewal

wafting through centuries:
  spring dancers, maypoles,
and all things paradisiacal.

Pink and Blue Dawn

Light reflects from pink
    stucco against blue sky.
It unfolds upward,
    a baby's blanket lifted:

soft cheek of morning
    peeping, uncovered.
Wisp of pink clouds pile,
    curled like tiny fingers,

peek-a-boo day begins.
    Cool air hovering,
gentle lips of day yawning,
    snuggle down:

pink and blue dawning,
    not yet morning.

"Finish Your Milk"

Milk spurts for a babe at her mother's breast.
It flows unceasingly until the need ceases.
It is a kind of libation for both,
delirious in each other's gaze.

Rocking, a first cradle, rosebud fists,
the first merger, mother and child,
bliss together, fuzzy head, soft warm round.
Stay a moment. Drink in.

Perfect harmony, the breast at the child's lips,
greedy sucking gone to rest, sufficient milk to each desire.
Rock, Mother, protect your flow, your dispensation,
your life's blood, your little love, your kindred soul.

"Finish your milk," Mother said to the growing child
to hold her close a moment longer. Too soon, too soon
she flies from her mother's breast, her mother's side,
her tiny feet pelting across the kitchen floor and out the open door.

Baby Talk

No operating instructions come with a dream.
My therapist offered a hint or two, said
a dream baby symbolizes the self,
a newborn thing, so I nibble on the image:
a baby—poor baby—dressed only
in a diaper, dragged around the dreamscape
like a doll forgotten at the first distraction.
He is soon dropped from a bridge, splash,
but rescued by a diver in full gear, this naked baby
who sees underwater, who swims like a dolphin.
Now he gurgles in an open car wash
where felt strips tickle him. Unperturbed,
he comes through like the real baby
born last week. A.J.'s mother passes him around
like a fancy hors d'oeuvre, his eyes new moon
slits, his sleep undisturbed. She has, no doubt,
fallen in love with him. I had no feeling
for him, for shame. My mother rocked
him and cooed; someone took their picture,
the one coming into life, the other slowly leaving.
A.J. came with no operating instructions,
no picture of a programming mode for his mother,
who, as I write this, is learning baby talk,
the language of love and full attention.

The Future

The fog slides in over quiet water, smothers sailboats,
swirls around them, obliterates them, turns the summer
afternoon into a winter day's mountaintop snow
adventure, the air white, white sound collapsed
into numbness, the mind of a fevered man lifts from sleep
in an unknown room where the calendar on the wall
changes at midnight, a new day beginning precisely
though he sleeps. A nurse in quiet shoes glides
around the chair with the dozing woman who remembers
the dream of two harbors both far below, one where light
reflected from the sides of hundreds of shimmering sardines
swirling like gathering mist, the other crammed
with whales, interwoven, interlocked, yin and yang, awesome
as the fog skimming in, filling a vacuum over the water,
just beginning to build a crystal barrier reflecting
sun as snow mounds do, as beautiful as the girl's long hair
swaying in sunlight, her life ahead of her, a line as broad
as the long harbor opening, as muffled and indistinct
as the fog fingers beckoning.

On the Loose

Look at the radiating swan feathers piled, then blown
apart in a swiftly created, swiftly deconstructed
montage on the sky.

This fluffy stuff, which might be an odd aging
hairdo on a blue skull won't stay tucked into place,
slips out of head bands and bobby pins to fly free

as a bird way high that floats
on M-shaped wings in the invisible wind.

Now the clouds tumble and weave, form
a geisha's hairdo, one so delicately piled,
the girl slept, her head resting on a wooden stand
so she wouldn't disturb her pinned and glued,
imprisoned locks.

Such movement of light and shape,
fragrance of wild narcissus in tall grass
entranced me until Father's two-fingered whistle
roused me to fly home like a cloud on scurrying feet.

What did I answer when he asked, *Where have you been?*

Mowing the Lawn

The lawn mower moved across the grass
in even patterns of order

disrupting moles and insects,
slugs and other bugs. As for slug me,

this morning a lawn mower shakes
me awake, sends me into paroxysms

of childhood—to tossing grass grenades
and burying each other in mounded graves.

The mower was a chunky, clunky thing
Dad oiled occasionally to ease

its path across the sea of grass,
its back and forth and back and forth.

One day he nearly died, it's true,
and tossed the family patterns all askew.

No more mowing, the doctor said,
so there we were my brother and I,

drafted into neatness feats, to pushing
the mower straight across the grass.

One night Dad roared, *Who cut my tree?*
Who nicked my elm? Ted taped

the wound, left the sore thumb tree
for all to see what a careless boy

he was. By then the rattletrap
mower was electrified, and now

my careless brother cut the cord,
so I became the family mower, smirking

back and forth and back and forth.
I loved to cut the grass, in bare feet—

beware—and thought I'd won
at pleasing Dad. My brother, though,

today would say: *A useless mower,
yes I was. My talent ran*

*more to cutting myself straight
out of a family work loop.*

Orleans Parade, July 4

This year I remember to set
cruise control so Aretha won't drive me
past the speed limit with her rhythmic
love lyrics that send shudders

of guilt through me as I remember
so many satisfying jumbles that lie
too deep inside, hidden in too many
nesting boxes to be sullied by mere expression.

My cousins put this family Fourth of July
celebration together so coherently:
People who bear little gifts arrive on time;
we park, then find our prearranged chairs

along the parade route; the children
don't cry or fall down. The Grand
Marshall appears, followed by the ramrod
veterans stepping lively step-in-step.

Much to my surprise I admire their discipline
in an understanding glimpse
of *sacrifice,* which I've earned by turning
off the stupid conversation in my head

that usually goes something like this:
*how could you go to war? how could you
kill someone? how could you give up
your only precious life?* Now I think

if anyone should go, everyone should go,
not just the warrior class, which may
or may not exist. Maybe *sacrifice* is lack of luck:
born in the wrong family, the wrong time,

the wrong town. A war flag flaps
endlessly somewhere, everywhere
to relieve boredom, land lust, vengeance.
And now here comes a band, so many grey heads

tromboning and trumpeting; then huge shiny red or yellow
fire engines, magnificent works of contemporary art,
all chrome and splendor; bagpipes that send
goose bumps along my arms. *Look*, I say

to my cousin, showing her how much I love them.
Have them at your funeral, she says. *Put it in your will.*
I'm so caught up in good feelings
that even the thought of my death brings

a smile at this idea dropped so nonchalantly
into the tangle of flying candies, children on bicycles,
women on the Willy's Gym float hefting
Styrofoam barbells, and dogs from the vet hospital

spaced just so, wearing their red silk lobster costumes.
I don't know how I came to be born
into this competent family when left field
is my home plate. Another family poet

scoots into the chair next to me
and confesses he's set six Gary Snyder poems
to music. I'm thrilled for him, didn't know he wrote
music. *He's my hero*, he says. *I sent them*

to him through a friend. I probably won't hear
from him, he adds, and I pat his knee,
deeply moved by a poet's challenges,
inside and outside our family.

A Swan Song for Shoestring Bay

So many swans appeared across the street—
not nine and fifty—but still they showed up
so suddenly.

Every day I nearly drive off the road
as I check to see what they are up to
with their wiry necks, their pouty beaks.

On its flat grey deck some days
they are scattered
like the unconnected dots of a terrorist plot.

Other days, feeding draws all heads and necks
below water, leaving the flat cove
studded with oval loaves of bread.

One day they will all disappear
with a smashing of wings against water,
then a quiet whir like an old fan.

Who is it if not me who has fallen asleep
and is now persuaded to pick up pen and begin?

Once I saw four flying majestically together
high overhead, soaring like ferocious ghosts.

I still swerve dangerously on the road,
head swiveling to see the spectacle

or hear, in the still of midnight,
a cacophony of honks
enough to wake the dead.

Voice from the Grave

i.
I don't have to eat here.
Sometimes where you are,
someone would force-feed me.

I was so angry.   It was *my* body.

I never expected Death
to take me so soon.

The doctor wept,
       but it wasn't his fault—

I didn't have a morsel of fat
to cushion my organs.

I was probably the oldest living anorexic
in the country—

      all 35 years of it.

I knew I couldn't stop,
but I didn't expect it would kill me.

ii.
I needed to be held,
just to be held.

So much therapy, so much talk.

At your friend's cabin in Tahoe,
I wanted to sleep in the same bed with you.
You probably thought
it was something sexual,
but I just wanted to be held,
my body was so cold.

We never talked about our bodies.
It was as though they didn't exist.
If they didn't exist, did we?

iii.
I learned in therapy
something happened.

I was too young when the housekeeper
started to care for me.

But my parents didn't know.
They did their best.

iv.
Why did you wait so long
to return to this town
        where we grew up?

What is this place
for you
        without me?

Remember
how our friends
        envied us?—

Remember
the prom—all those godawful
blue and yellow crepe flowers:

Hawaiian Dream Song
        or some such thing.

I looked like Sandra Dee
and you looked like Little Lost
Alice Blue Gown.

And that hairdresser!
Remember how she said to me

You will go far with those eyes.

v.
My father used to ask
about our friends,
took me into the piano room,
quizzed me after dates.

Did your father do that?

When Susan got pregnant
      he was apoplectic.

*What kind of girls
are your friends, anyway?*

vi.
My disease started in New York.
I was afraid to cab
      across Central Park at night,

wanted to stay in our apartment,
      talk to our neighbors.

They told me they were too old for me,

I would find someone,
      but I never did.

One day a thin stranger
stopped me on the street:

      You have it, too.

I looked up 'anorexic'
in the dictionary.

vii.
When I grocery shopped for my family,
Mother would laugh to her friends:

> *She bought me blueberry muffins.*
> *She has a relationship with the muffin lady,*
> *who takes out a sample for her to try*
> *right from the oven.*

You were frustrated shopping with me,
checking every expiration date.
      I couldn't help it.

San Francisco's Marina Safeway was the best,
with its papayas and plump strawberries,
      the view of the harbor.

I might have moved to San Francisco,
just for that store—

and our friendship, of course.

viii.
I know you chose great restaurants
when I visited.

At Opera Plaza when
I saw your salad, I wanted it.

Then the fish
in that dark restaurant
with all the contemporary art
we couldn't see.

They told us over the phone the chef
would bake the sole *without* butter
and it came *drenched* in butter.

Then you started to cry. Why?

ix.
Do you think I helped my little ones enough?
Some of them had only me—so many parents on drugs.

I let them hang out in my office.
Anthony—big eyes, big smile, big sense of humor—
    broke   my heart.

Was it better to take him away
from his parents?

You were shocked at my stories.
Our quiet village changed horribly.

A teacher committed suicide.
I organized grief sessions.
What could I say?

I was engaged,
but you always seemed so detached.

x.
Thank you for sitting with my family
and for coming to say good-bye.

Did the superintendent
write his eulogy?

I never stood up
in someone's red convertible,
proclaiming:
    Live your life now.

Why didn't you read your wonderful poem,
"Keep the Conversation Going"?
    It meant a lot to me.

You're too reticent.
I'm glad you write poetry;
some things slip out.

I saw you searching for my grave.
Did you really think

    at last you rest in peace.

Variations of these poems first appeared in the following journals:

Cape Cod Poetry Review: "Catastrophic Expectations," "Swan Song for Shoestring Bay"

Naugatuck River Review: "Orleans Parade, July 4"

Pudding: "A Protestant Mourns Sensations Lost"

Rattle: "Moments"

Sahara, a Journal of New England Poetry: "Expression on Time's Face," "coming of age," "Secrets"

Slant: "Shadows on the Screen," "Baby Talk"

World of Water, World of Sand, a Cape Cod collection of poetry, fiction and memoir: "Caesar Musing after Meeting Cleopatra"

About the Author

Judith Askew has been writing poetry for over four decades. She has worked as an editor and writer in several corporate settings and was founder and publisher of a women's health newsletter. Her writing career began during her college years at *The Barnstable Patriot,* where she wrote a column and articles during her summer break. Askew also co-edited *Out of the Cellar,* an anthology of women's poems (D'Aurora Press), in the early 1970s. Her first collection of poetry, *Here at the Edge of the Sea,* was published by Artship Publishing in 2009. Before focusing on her own poetry, Askew taught developmental writing for eight years as an adjunct professor at Cape Cod Community College. She currently lives in Cotuit, MA.

People are already talking about *On the Loose*...

"Think how much fun it would be to meet someone for lunch who'd talk about Claes Oldenburg's giant clothes pins; Robert Bly's poem on clothes pins; her (very different) grandmothers' attitudes towards laundry; her memories of strange things seen on laundry lines over the years; and, just when you're about to condemn the conversation for being alluringly yet frivolously amusing, a brief frown, and the sobering apercu that we're hanging, all of us, on laundry lines ourselves and could at any time 'fall out of history' along with the silly, near-obsolescent clothes pins. Because these poems don't seem to take themselves too seriously, they feel like a conversation—free-floating, often concerned with everyday issues—with a friend willing to talk about almost anything that comes into her head, skipping around (as if to prove you're getting all her thoughts as she's thinking them, not just the censored acceptable ones) and yet, quite often, delivering a momentary gust of wisdom, dark agnosticism, and even scathing indictment to remind you you're not really in a completely safe place, but with someone unafraid and even willing, without warning, to face terror. Treat yourself to this book. The companionship of Judith Askew is delightful and instructive too, and *On the Loose* represents her finest poetry to date."
-Alan Feldman, author of *A Sail to Great Island* and *Happy Genius*

"Watching a young mother learning to speak in 'baby talk,' Judith Askew remarks that this mother is learning the 'language of love and full attention.' Poetry speaks its own ever-evolving, increasingly complex dialect of love and attention, and *On the Loose* offers us this poet's eloquent yet down-to-earth evocation of the predicaments and dilemmas of life in our time, especially those faced by women. Here are poems that address the 'secrets' of a girl's coming of age, the enchantments of Eros, and the negotiations of adult responsibilities to aspects of self and others. Here also are poems that confront our mortal limits, yet all the while keep in mind the beauty we dwell within. And most of all, here are poems that take the measure of our fundamental human desire for connection and the equally strong yearning of the spirit to be utterly free. Blake tells us that eternity is in love with the products of time. Judith Askew's poetry helps us understand why."
-Fred Marchant, author of *The Looking House* and *Tipping Point*

"*On the Loose* is a collection of poems full of distinctive wit and nine kinds of liveliness-- intellectual, emotional, sexual, plaintive, and otherwise. The poet consistently finds quick and original speech for the particularities of our human condition, and she is full of witty self-perspective as well. *On the Loose* covers all the rites of passage, including loss and sorrow, but a tone of genuine amusement and the resourceful idiom to make it believable are its reliable poetic allies. Full of pleasure and sensibility, this is a book that will make its readers happy."
-Tony Hoagland, author of *Donkey Gospel* and *What Narcissism Means to Me*

www.ingramcontent.com/pod-product-compliance
Lightning Source LLC
Chambersburg PA
CBHW072108290426

44110CB00014B/1867